Verses ♥ of Happiness

Debasish Mridha, M.D.
Edited by Sue Wolfe

Epitome Publishing
Copyright 2016

ISBN 978-0-9982426-0-6

Verses of Happiness

One thing all human beings seem to be looking for is happiness. What is happiness? What makes us happy? How do we find happiness in our everyday lives? These are questions that I have been asking myself as I study the world's most famous philosophers.

In this book *Verses of Happiness,* I am sharing with you, my dear readers, my most profound thoughts on happiness. I hope that these quotes and the accompanying artwork will inspire you to bring happiness into your everyday thoughts and actions.

As you learn to change your perceptions and actions to produce happiness in your life, it is my most sincere hope that this happiness will spill over into your heart and help humanity to be filled with peace, love, and happiness.

Dear Reader,

Studying philosophy is a passion and a mission of my life. I am searching for the deepest truths of life. Writing has become my way of exploring the deeply driving desires of the human mind.

I have lived in many countries and many cultures. I have been poor and I have been wealthy. I found that the pursuit of happiness is not different in different cultures or different social statuses. The question is the same for everyone. How do I create happiness in my life? I have decided that bringing happiness to the lives of others is my ultimate passion of life. It is my mission to increase the awareness of happiness, to change the thought processes concerning happiness, and to change perceptions so that we may allow happiness into our lives and into humanity.

While thinking about the ultimate passion of life, my thoughts began to focus on finding the reason and purpose of happiness. The quotes contained in this book are a few of my most favorite quotes that I have written about happiness.

My purpose in sharing these thoughts with you is to inspire you to find happiness in your life. The journey to happiness begins with changing your thoughts and perceptions of the world so that you may fill your heart with the warm comfort of happiness. It is my utmost desire that this book will guide you and sustain you in your journey toward happiness in your life.

It is my utmost desire that this book will guide you and sustain you in your journey toward a lifetime of happiness.

– Debasish Mridha, M.D.

Service is *joy*
Service is *kindness*
Service is *love*
Service is *happiness*

I am a **great success**, not because of what I have, but because I have found enduring **happiness** through the service to others.

Happiness is the appreciation of what you have- not what you should have.

Never pursue happiness, just create the happiness **inside** you.

Our happiness should not depend on external things; happiness is the expression of **internal attitudes.**

8

The ultimate purpose of our life is to be happy.

We are born for happiness; we are going toward happiness.
We like to live in happiness, and we like to vanish
from this universe into eternal happiness.

When you serve humanity and contribute to society **without expectation**, you will be happy.

Happiness absolutely
depends on
how you think.

No matter where we are coming
from, where we live, or
whatever we do, we all have the
same purpose in life; that is
to be happy.

11

When you are
non-judgmental you are happ

Happiness depends on you:
on your thoughts, on your
attitude, on your ideas,
on your vision
and on nothing else.

12

Happiness is there when you are **morally clear** to yourself.

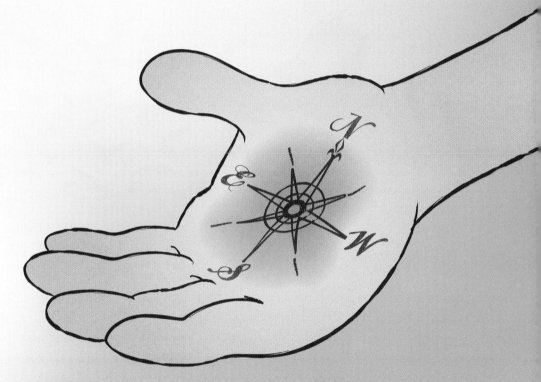

To fulfill our lives and be happy, we have to enjoy the little things.

We must **see the beauty** around us now instead of waiting for big things to enjoy.

Otherwise happiness will just pass us by while we wait for something else to come along.

I am responsible for my life, my happiness, and my joy. I am responsible for my faults which I will work to destroy.

Your life **really begins** when you learn to realize that no one else but you is responsible for your **amazing life**.

When you engage in
work that you love,
you are **happy.**

I dwell in
happiness
to find myself.

When you learn to enjoy every little event and you learn to see **beauty in every little thing,** you will enter the door of eternal happiness.

Share your *love*.

Share your **happiness**.

Care for **others**.

Do these three things and your
wealth will be endless.

To be happy, be the cause
of happiness for others.

I am happy because my **happiness** does
not depend on things but on my **thoughts**.

Happiness is the gap between
longing and *loving*.

If we had the chance to *live* forever,
life would lose its charm while we
waited for something better.

When we learn to enjoy
failure as well as **success**,
we will be eternally happy
and *joyful* for sure.

Happiness resides in your mind.

Never infect your mind with negative
thoughts or happiness will fly away.

Make **inner peace** your final
destination. Make **happiness**
your life's purpose.

Whenever you **smile,**

whenever you **care,**

whenever you **love,**

because **happiness** will be there.

your spirit will dance with **joy**

whenever you **share,**

24

Loving, caring,
and the spirit
of kindness always
bring **happiness**.

Our greatest
happiness depends
on what we love, how
we **care**, and
how we **share**.

When my heart is full of **love**
and kindness, I see **joy** and
kindness all around me.

Let happiness bloom in the freshness of your mind

In the **gentle wind**
  of your thoughts

On the **ground**
  of kindness and
  compassion

Let happiness **bloom** in the carefree love

In the **softness** of your tender voice

In the nonjudgmental **love**

In the **beauty** and **pureness**
  of a smile

Everything you do, do for happiness.

You will find that you are a great success.

A little **sadness** shows the way to happiness.
A little **kindness** can heal the sadness.

Don't wait!

Be happy every moment because every moment is precious and magical.

What others think does not matter.

What you think about **yourself** is what matters.

If you have to think, think of **beauty** and **happiness.**

The garden of **happiness** has no room to grow a weed like resentment.

31

My happiness comes from the many donations of my **time** and **talents** to benefit the current and future generations.

Find a place to **think** and a person to **love** and you will be happy.

The only way to find happiness is to make **someone else** happy.

In the wilderness of life
Happiness is looking for you:

In the jungles of dreams and
desires
In the beauty of shrubs and
flowers
In the span of sadness and
kindness
In the deepness of
hearts and *minds*.

In the garden of my heart

Flowers of love are blooming

Not just to express beauty

But to spread the

fragrance of happiness.

Where there is _love_ you will find
the nectar and happiness of life.

You are happy only when you spread the seeds of happiness around.

Happiness will grow if you plant the seeds
of **love** in the garden of **hope** and water
with **compassion** and **care**.

Even when I was a very young man, I was looking for the purpose of life.

I was looking for happiness all over the world: in fame and glamour, in wealth and splendor. I did not know how foolish I was. Happiness is not out there. Happiness is *inside* of me, in my **mind,** in my **thoughts.** Happiness is in my **perception** of the world.

Happiness has no book value, but life has no value if there is no happiness.

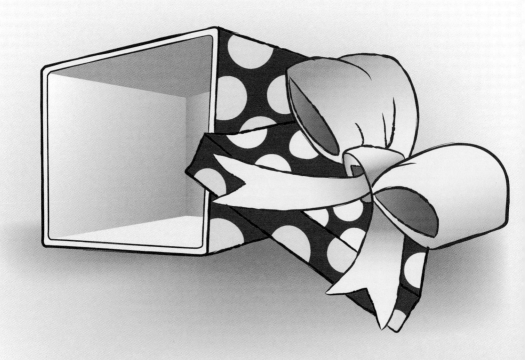

The only way to find happiness is to be
simple and *love* every moment and everything.

Finding the **happiness** within
is difficult but looking for
happiness outside is futile.

39

Why are you choosing to be unhappy when you were created for **happiness?**

Happiness is there where wants and needs are small but the desire to give is **big.**

It is what you think, not what you achieve, that makes you **happy.**

Three things will
make you happy:

always have **happy** thoughts,
be *honest* with yourself,
and express unconditional *love* for everything

42

Feel freely, dance freely, smile softly, sing sweetly, love endlessly and be happy always.

Just be happy because you are reading me.

You are alive!

Children are happy because they have the power of finding happiness in the **simplest of things.**

The secret of a **happy life** is to live a life with child-like simplicity, appreciate nature's **beauty** and admire **honesty.**

Happiness is an inner perception, inner joyfulness.

We are happy when we express our kindness unconditionally.

We are happy when we love someone *unconditionally.*
By becoming the source of happiness for someone we become happy.
Happiness is the purpose of every creation.

Never try to be happy, but always try to
make someone happy.

All the happiness in the world will be yours.

Every morning the sun is **smiling**
over the horizon of life to see us happy.

Oh! Happiness

I am looking for you
In the wilderness
In and around the palaces
In my possessions
In my wealth and splendor.

I can see you far away
Like an illusion
I try to touch, feel, and smell
But like a mirage, you dance far away.

47

Happiness will come today,
tomorrow, and every year
Now, then and every moment
For if we learn to love, care, and share

Happiness will come
To fill our heart with kindness
It is a gift from the universe
To touch our life with joyful silence

Happiness will come
If we know wealth and splendor are an illusion
But the attainment of a mental state of happiness
And unconditional love is a real possession
Happiness will come

48

If **success** is the flower of life, then happiness is the fragrance of those flowers.

Let it go with *love* so that you may grow and be happy.

A simple **act of kindness** could be the source of great happiness.

Happiness is not always found in success,
but **success** is always found in happiness.

Choose to be **someone** not just anyone.

Whenever you **feel** me, just **call** me with the silence of your soul and the softness of your love. I will be with you.

With the **magic** of my love you may not see me but you will feel me.

You will hear my song in the depth of your **heart** you will **hear** me.

Kindness is like sunshine; it can warm up and *enlighten* every heart.

Every morning, the sun is inviting you to open
the window, join the party, and be happy.

You have to live with
yourself for the rest of your life.
So like yourself. Love
yourself. Do only those things
which make you
proud of yourself.

Do only those things which
make humanity proud of you.

54

Giving back is the greatest
gift of love for humanity and
the greatest source of joy in life.

The value of a life
does not depend on how
much you are making.

It depends on how much you are sharing.

When you **create opportunities** for others the whole world becomes your window of opportunity.

Carry some burdens for others; you will be **stronger** and **happier.**

Be a human angel!

With love, generosity and kindness, let us lighten
the burden of suffering from our fellow man.

We often concentrate on the negative side of humanity, **but humanity is growing, maturing every day, and singing a song of a better future.**

With a **smile,** every morning drink a cup of sunshine to fill your heart with happiness.

Let us help each other.
Let us serve each other.
Let us be kind to each other.
Let us be compassionate to each other.
Let us love humanity and love each other.

Heavenly thoughts
come floating into my mind
like waves of lights with bright
color and beauty to brighten
my life with delight.

Every morning, look a
the magnificent sun
and fill your heart wit
golden rays
of happiness.

60

A simple dream, a simple thought, can generate actions to shake the world.

Life is a gift, so enjoy
the delight of opening the
gift every day!

Life expands when you dare and share.
Life shrinks when you seek consistency and fear.
Spirit is the source of life.
In growth, resides seeds of happiness.
So always take action for spiritual growth
and eternal happiness.

Your attitude toward life is
more important than environment,
upbringing, and even your education.

So always have a happy positive attitude.

If you feel that you touched one heart, if you feel that you improved one life, if you feel that you enjoyed the beauty of nature, then *life* was worth living.

The measure of life is not what you have done for yourself, but what you have *done for others.*

Life is a journey; love is the way;
happiness is the goal.

Your life has many
purposes, many goals, but the
ultimate purpose
of life is to be happy.

I want to waste my life
Just by thinking
Just by writing
Just by dreaming my life.

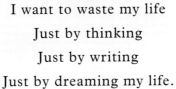

I want to spend my life
Just by loving
Just by caring
Just by sharing my life.

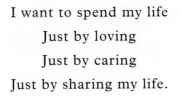

I want to destroy my life
Just by giving
Just by forgiving
Just by living my life.

Be grateful
because you are
blessed with life.

You are alive.
You are going through the most
amazing journey we call life. The
universe has been waiting for your
smile for billions of years. How can you
not be happy today?

I **appreciate** all the beauty, all
the love, all the joy and all the little
wonders and charm around me.

The universe is a mirror;

however you look at it, it will look back at you exactly the same way. So extend your hand with love. The universe will hug you with a loving heart.

69

Make *enthusiasm* a way of life.

Make **optimism** a way of success.

Make *gratitude* a way of happiness.

A simple thought can transform you forever.
So cultivate **beautiful thoughts**
always, ugliness never.

Think your best thoughts every moment, every day.
You will be the best person on the way.

You cannot go back and start a brand new beginning,

But today is a new day and you can start a brand new thing.

WELCOME

Life is short. Fill it with love, joy, and happiness.

You are the creator of your thoughts,
   Thoughts create your actions,
      and actions create YOU.

Forgive yourself to create
yourself again and again.

The biggest mistake in life is not to make one.
The biggest risk in life is being afraid to take one.

He who gives away an **abundance of love** and possesses an attitude of gratitude is always happy.

One life, one love, one desire –
happiness.

Acknowledgments

I wish to personally thank my beautiful wife and wonderful daughter for teaching me about true happiness and for their love and support which brings me happiness and joy every day.

I wholeheartedly appreciate Sue Wolfe for her tireless editing and proofreading of this book. Her hard work has helped to enhance the overall purpose and content of this book.

I would also like to thank Jerry Langmaid for the beautiful artwork that reveals the essence of *Verses of Happiness.*

I also want to thank my staff for keeping me organized and on track: Lisa MacArthur, Heather Kehoe, April Neumann, and Sudip Malakar.

78

About the Author

Dr. Debasish Mridha

Dr. Debasish Mridha, is an American physician, philosopher, poet seer, and author. He is a seeker of the deepest truth that affects human destiny. His empowering, insightful, thought-provoking, and life changing words have been changing human conscience every day.

I am a humble man from a distant land,
From the core of my heart, I love you all,
I may not be able to touch you with my hand,
I am sending you flowers of love,
Wishing you the brightness of the sun,
Calmness and beauty of the moon,
And touching your heart,
Through these verses of happiness and love.

– *Debasish Mridha, M.D.*